What does it mean to have

Asthma

Louise Spilsbury

Heinemann LIBRARY

www.heinemann.co.uk/library
Visit our website to find out more information about Heinemann Library books.

To order:
 Phone 44 (0) 1865 888066
 Send a fax to 44 (0) 1865 314091
Visit the Heinemann Bookshop at www.heinemann.co.uk/library to browse our catalogue and order online.

First published in Great Britain by Heinemann Library,
Halley Court, Jordan Hill, Oxford OX2 8EJ,
a division of Reed Educational and Professional Publishing Ltd.
Heinemann is a registered trademark of Reed Educational and Professional Publishing Ltd.

OXFORD MELBOURNE AUCKLAND
JOHANNESBURG BLANTYRE GABORONE
IBADAN PORTSMOUTH (NH) USA CHICAGO

Designed by AMR
Illustrated by Art Construction
Originated by Dot Gradations
Printed by Wing King Tong, Hong Kong.

ISBN 0 431 13920 2 (hardback)   ISBN 0 431 13927 X (paperback)
06 05 04 03 02   06 05 04 03 02
10 9 8 7 6 5 4 3 2   10 9 8 7 6 5 4 3 2 1

British Library Cataloguing in Publication Data
Spilsbury, Louise
   What does it mean to have asthma?
   1.Asthma
   I.Title II.Asthma
   616.2'38

Acknowledgements
The Publishers would like to thank the following for permission to reproduce photographs:
John Birdsall Photography, p.23; Rebecca Huxley, pp.12, 13; National Asthma Campaign, p.11; Powerstock Zefa/Benelux Press, p.5; Science Photo Library/Mark Clarke, p.4, /Andrew Syred, p.26; Tony Stone Images/Lori Adamski Peek, p.24, /Bill Aron, p.22, /Nello Giambi, p.8, /David Hanover, p.10, /Howard Kingsnorth, p.27, /Simon Jauncey, p.9; John Walsmley, p.25.

The following pictures were taken on commission:
Gareth Boden, pp.16, 28, 29; Trevor Clifford, pp.15, 17, 18; John Walmsley, pp.14, 19, 20, 21.

The pictures on the following pages were posed by models who do not have asthma:
4–5, 10, 14–15, 17–25, 27.

Special thanks to:
Elizabeth, Emma, Natasha, Philip, Rupert, Sam, Saqib, Sebastian.

The publishers would also like to thank the National Asthma Campaign; also Julie Johnson, PHSE Consultant, Trainer and Writer.

Cover photograph reproduced with permission of Action Plus.

Every effort has been made to contact copyright holders of any material reproduced in this book. Any omissions will be rectified in subsequent printings if notice is given to the publishers.

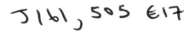

Children with asthma

Around one in seven children have asthma. So, if you have asthma, you are probably not the only person in your class to have it. You will not be able to tell if someone has asthma just by looking at them. Most children with asthma are able to keep their asthma under control and get on with leading full and active lives, just like everyone else.

Children who have asthma should not have to miss out on school or any other activity. They can keep their asthma under control and get on with making the most of their lives.

Facts about asthma
- Asthma is a major cause of ill health, especially among children.
- Around one in seven children have asthma.
- Over 100 million people across the world have asthma.
- Asthma affects about one in twenty people in the UK.
- The number of people who have asthma is increasing.

How we breathe

To understand asthma, you need to know a bit about the **lungs** and the way we breathe. Breathing is the way **air** is pushed in and out of your lungs. Your lungs are in your chest. They are connected to your throat by a tube called the windpipe, or trachea. The air you breathe is sucked up your nose or into your mouth, down your windpipe and into your lungs.

The lungs are made up of a series of tubes. The proper name for these **airways** is **bronchi**. The air travels through the bronchi to bunches of air sacs called alveoli. These fill up with air like tiny balloons. Then **oxygen** from the air passes through the alveoli walls and into your blood.

When you breathe air into your lungs, oxygen passes into the blood. The blood then carries the oxygen around the body to where it is needed.

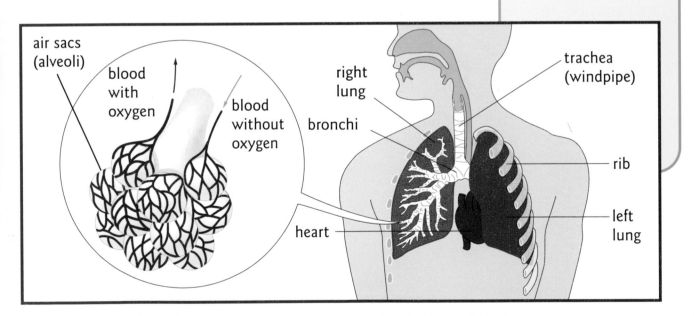

air sacs (alveoli)

blood with oxygen

blood without oxygen

right lung

bronchi

heart

trachea (windpipe)

rib

left lung

Why do we breathe?

We breathe all the time because our bodies need a regular supply of oxygen. Oxygen is a gas that is in the air all around us. Oxygen helps our bodies turn the food we eat into energy. We need energy for everything we do – to live, move and grow.

Asthma and airways

Asthma is a disease that affects the bronchi (airways). Children who have asthma have bronchi that are usually red, swollen and sensitive, or **inflamed**. This may not bother them most of the time. However, when something happens to irritate the bronchi, such as catching a cold or breathing in smoke, an **asthma attack** can happen.

In an asthma attack, the lining of the bronchi starts to swell. This means there is less room for air to get through. The muscles around the walls of the tubes also become tighter. This makes the tubes even narrower and it becomes harder to breathe. Sometimes the airways also fill with **mucus**. This is the sticky stuff your throat produces when you get a cold. This means that the person with asthma may also start wheezing and coughing.

Asthma **symptoms** can be soothed quickly with special medicines. These relax the muscles in the bronchi so that they become wide enough for air to pass through again. They also reduce any swelling.

In an asthma attack, the lining of the bronchi starts to swell, the muscles tighten and mucus may be made.

People without asthma have airways like this:

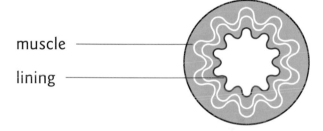

muscle

lining

People with asthma have airways like this:

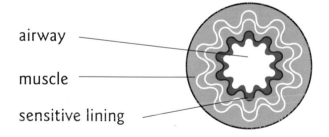

airway

muscle

sensitive lining

This is what happens in an asthma attack:

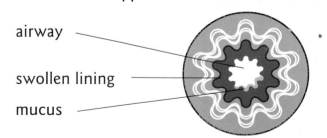

airway

swollen lining

mucus

What causes an asthma attack?

An **asthma attack** happens when a child with asthma comes into contact with an asthma **trigger**. A trigger is anything that irritates the airways and causes the **symptoms** of asthma to appear – coughing, wheezing, shortness of breath or a tight feeling in the chest. There are many different triggers that can cause an attack.

Everyone's asthma is different. Every child with asthma has a different set of triggers that start an asthma attack. Most people who have asthma have mild asthma and are good at controlling it. Even so, they might still have an asthma attack once in a while.

Allergies

Many children who have asthma also have **allergies**. An allergy happens when their body's **immune system** reacts to something in the **environment**. Children with allergies react badly to things, like dust or pet hair, which do not usually cause reactions in other children. Allergic reactions may include asthma symptoms, or may just cause sneezing, watery eyes or a runny nose. The substance, or thing, that a person is allergic to is called an **allergen**.

*Some people think that worsening air **pollution** from smoke and fumes from traffic and factories can make asthma worse. They say it is also partly responsible for the increase in the number of children with asthma.*

Asthma triggers

These are some of the triggers that cause most asthma problems.

- Colds, flu and other **viruses** and **bacteria** – Viral infections of the **respiratory** (breathing) system are the worst culprits. In winter, around eight out of ten children who visit hospital because of asthma attacks have viral infections such as colds or flu.

- House-dust mites – These tiny insects live mainly in carpets, beds and sofas. Their droppings cause problems for many people with asthma.

- Cigarettes – Cigarette smoke makes a lot of people with asthma cough and feel out of breath.

- Furry or feathery animals – Pets such as birds, cats and dogs can cause asthma attacks.

- Pollen – In summer, flowers and grasses release pollen, which helps plants make seeds to grow into new plants. Pollen can cause asthma in some people. It also causes a related problem, called **hay fever**.

- Exercise – Some people have to be careful of doing certain kinds of strenuous exercise, especially on cold, dry days.

- Weather – Sudden changes in the weather or temperature can worsen asthma symptoms for some people.

Most people love the sight of spring and summer flowers in grassy meadows. However, for some children with asthma, they are a nuisance. Pollen from flowers and grasses is a trigger for half of all people with asthma.

How do people know they have asthma?

There is no simple test that a doctor can do to find out whether someone has asthma or not. This is partly because the **symptoms** of asthma vary from person to person. One person with asthma may always have a wheezy cough, whereas another may have trouble breathing now and again. It is also tricky to **diagnose** (say for sure someone has) asthma because the symptoms may be similar to other breathing disorders. For example, a person may have difficulty breathing because they have a chest infection, not asthma. Most children have early warning signs, such as a tight feeling in their chest. Their doctor carries out detailed investigations to find out if asthma is the cause.

For a very small number of people, their first sign of a problem may be a bad **asthma attack**. They may have to go to hospital for treatment. With help they can get the asthma under control.

Once a doctor has diagnosed asthma, children can begin treatment to control the symptoms and make them feel well again.

At the doctor's

Doctors and other health workers have to do a number of things to find out if a person has asthma. First they weigh and measure the patient and find out their medical history. This is a record of any health problems they have had in the past. Everyone has a health record like this. It is usually kept at your doctor's or your health clinic.

Then the doctor finds out about the patient's family medical history. Asthma often runs in families and may be **inherited**. This means that if there are people in the patient's family who have asthma, the patient is more likely to have asthma as well.

Peak flow meter

The doctor may measure a patient's breathing with a **peak flow meter**. This is a special device that measures how hard someone can blow air out of their **lungs**. When they blow into it, a marker slides up a scale. If someone's breathing level is lower than normal, it can mean they have asthma. As their asthma improves with treatment, they are able to blow out harder and their peak flow scores are higher.

*Peak flow meters measure how hard people can breathe out. If someone cannot breathe out hard, it means his or her **airways** may be narrow because of asthma.*

Meet Philip

My name is Rebecca, and I'm Philip's mum. Philip is eight years old now, but was **diagnosed** as having asthma when he was nearly two years old. It was quite unusual for someone to be diagnosed with asthma that young. Although it was scary and I was very worried about Philly, in some ways it was a relief when we were told. He had been quite ill up to that time and no one seemed to be able to do anything about it. He cried all the time, had been sick a lot and hardly slept. Then he was taken to hospital. After coming out of hospital with the right asthma medicines, things improved a lot. Philly slept, was not sick and did not cry as much.

The first years were difficult and I was worried about him all the time. He has one brother and two sisters and I often felt that they didn't get the attention they deserved because I had to spend a lot of time with Philly, taking him to the doctor's and giving him his medicine. Even though his asthma is quite severe, it is now under control, and our lives are a lot easier.

My name is Philip. My asthma can be annoying. I have to take medicine all the time and sometimes I can't keep up with my friends when I'm not well. I'm also a bit smaller than the other boys in my class because of the asthma. Some people tease me and think I'm younger than I am. Being a bit small also means I can't go on all the rides at the funfair that I want because I'm under the height they

say you have to be. I don't like coughing at night-time because it keeps me awake and I get tired.

I like going to the hospital for check-ups. They are fine and the people there are nice. I also get an afternoon off school when I go for a check-up. It's OK at school. Everyone knows I have asthma, and the teachers know what to do if I feel ill. I can do exactly the same as everyone else most of the time. But I know when I need to sit quietly for a while.

Coping with asthma

There are no wonder pills to cure asthma completely and no guarantees that a child with asthma will grow out of it, though this can happen. Even so, most children with asthma don't let it stop them from getting on with their lives. How do they do it? There are two key tactics children have for coping with asthma. The first is treating the **symptoms**, by taking medicines regularly, at the times and in the amounts **prescribed** by a doctor. The second is learning what causes their **asthma attacks** so they can reduce or avoid those **triggers**.

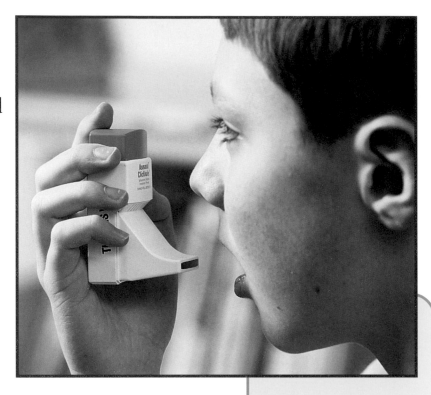

Children with asthma take their medicine through an inhaler, which they put right in their mouth. The inhaler helps them take the right amount of medicine easily.

Treating the symptoms

There are several different kinds of medicine that are used to treat asthma. They can be divided into two main kinds – **relievers** and **preventers**. The two kinds work in different ways, but both are usually taken by the same method. They are inhaled, which means they are breathed in. **Inhalers** are a really effective way of taking asthma medicine because it goes straight to where it is needed most – the **airways** inside your **lungs**.

Identifying triggers

Some children have asthma triggers that are easy to spot. They may always start wheezing or coughing after they have touched a dog or been in the same room as one. For others, though, it can be hard to find out exactly what brings on an asthma attack. These children may need to do some serious detective work to find their triggers.

The best way for a child to discover what sets off their asthma attacks is to keep a diary. In it, they keep a careful note of when their asthma symptoms get worse. They record the time of day, what they have just been doing, or eating, and where they have been. After a while, a pattern may emerge. It may become clear, for instance, that an asthma attack always happens when the child plays football on cold winter days or after visiting a grandparent's house where there is a cat. Once a child knows what sets off asthma, they can lessen the chance of an attack by avoiding those triggers.

Cold air is a trigger for around six out of ten people who have asthma. Wearing a thick scarf wrapped around your nose and mouth can help, as this warms up the air before it is breathed in.

Medication is important!

The most important part of controlling asthma is taking the right medication at the right time. Everyone's asthma is different. Each person needs different kinds of medicine, at different times and in different amounts. Some children may only need to use **reliever** medicines, but others need to use both **preventer** and reliever medicines.

Reliever medicines

Reliever medicines are the ones children take to stop (relieve) the **symptoms** of an **asthma attack**. Relievers work quickly to relax the muscles around the **airways**. As the muscles relax, the airways become wider. This makes it easier for air to pass through and it becomes easier to breathe again. Some people with mild asthma only get asthma symptoms once or twice a week, perhaps after games at school. If their asthma does not bother them the rest of the time, they can probably get by with a few puffs from a reliever **inhaler** when they need it.

Reliever and preventer inhalers are usually different colours. This means people can tell at a glance which is which. That is important because they may need to grab a reliever quickly if they have an asthma attack.

Preventer medicines

Preventer medicines have to be taken regularly because they work over a long period of time. They are no use if someone is already having an attack. Their job is to help the airways to calm down and become less **inflamed** (red and sore) over time. When the airways are less inflamed, they are less likely to react badly if they come into contact with an asthma **trigger**.

Children use preventer inhalers every day, usually first thing in the morning and last thing at night. The important thing about preventer medicines is that children need to take them all the time – even when they are feeling well.

Children with asthma carry their inhalers with them wherever they go because they never know when they might need them. Some make special bags to keep them in, or they carry them in bum-bags.

Spacers

Spacers are special devices that help the medicine in an inhaler go straight to the airways. Spacers are large plastic containers with a mouthpiece at one end and a hole for the inhaler to fit in at the other end. Spacers help children with asthma use their inhalers more easily, and they stop the medicine making their throat feel dry.

Check-ups

Children with asthma have regular check-ups, to keep a check on how their asthma is. Their doctor or nurse weighs and measures them. If they are growing steadily, it is a sign that they are healthy. They also have a medical check-up to make sure their throat and **lungs** are all right. Check-ups are also a chance for children to chat to the doctor about how they are feeling and to ask any questions they might have.

Keeping a diary as a record of their symptoms helps children keep a check on their own asthma.

Taking care of yourself

Children with asthma also take a lot of the responsibility themselves for checking on their asthma. Many keep diaries of their asthma **symptoms**. They record what medicines they are taking and how they are feeling. They may also include readings from a **peak flow meter**.

Lots of children have their own peak flow meters at home. If their peak flow reading drops below a certain level which they have agreed beforehand with their doctor, it means their asthma may be getting out of control. They know it is time for a visit to a clinic for some help with getting back on top of the asthma.

Treating an asthma attack

Sometimes, even when children are very good at controlling their asthma, they may have an **asthma attack**. If a child in your school has an asthma attack, there is no need to panic. There are a few simple steps to follow.

1 The child should use their **reliever inhaler** straightaway.

2 You should tell an adult that the child is not feeling well. It is very important to do this – even if you feel it is embarrassing to break up a lesson or interrupt a teacher.

3 The child should sit down and try to keep calm. This may be tough if they are feeling bad, but it helps if they and the people around them stay calm.

4 After about five or ten minutes the reliever should have worked and they should be feeling much better. They can carry on with what they were doing before the attack.

5 On the few occasions that the reliever inhaler is not enough, a child may have to see a doctor who can get their asthma back under control.

Meet Kevin

I started to have asthma when I was eight years old. I'm eleven now. When I first found out, I got really down about it. I thought it might stop me doing the things I liked, like playing football. Luckily the doctor I saw at our clinic was really cool. He spent hours talking to me. He had asthma too and it hadn't stopped him doing anything. We worked together to find the medicines that suited me best. And he helped me see that I could find ways of controlling my asthma, rather than it controlling me!

Colds and flu or animal hair used to really set my asthma off. It got quite bad whenever I caught a cold. I'd start wheezing and couldn't stop. I had to go to hospital a couple of times. But now the asthma is pretty much under control. I use my **preventer inhaler** every day – mornings before school, and evenings before bed – and my **reliever** inhaler when I feel a bit wheezy. But that doesn't happen very often. I'm a lot happier now my asthma has improved.

As well as taking my medicines every day, even when I'm feeling good, I avoid the things that set me off. My best friend's got this furball of a cat and it was hard for me to visit him because the fluff everywhere set my asthma off again. Now he keeps his cat out of his room, so that I can go round to his house to see him. And I always take my reliever inhaler with me, just in case.

All my friends know about my asthma. They all know what to do if I have an **asthma attack** and where I keep my spare inhaler at school, so they can help me out if I need them to. I always tell people I have asthma. It's safer if they know what to do if I have an attack. But I don't want them to treat me differently. I just want to get on with doing the things I enjoy, like playing with the boy next door.

Sometimes the asthma can be a bit of a pain. Like on really cold, winter days. Once or twice I've had to stop playing football for a while and rest, or just give it a miss for a few days. But otherwise I pretty much do anything I want.

Living with asthma

One person's asthma may be very different to someone else's. Some children grow out of their asthma. Some people develop asthma again later in life, while others have asthma **symptoms** throughout their life.

For some children with mild asthma, it does not interfere with their life at all. For others, it may be something they have to be aware of all the time. Most people with asthma find ways of living with their asthma which allow them to control it, rather than the other way around.

How does it feel?

If you ask them, many children say they would rather not have to live with the inconveniences of asthma. Most, though, just accept it and take it in their stride. Some even say that their asthma has made a positive difference to their life. They say that having asthma means they take better care of their health because they try to keep fit and well. To manage asthma well, you also have to be pretty strict with yourself. Many children find this makes them more capable and independent.

Some young people with asthma say that it has made them more determined to get on with things and make the most of their life.

Getting away – school trips and holidays

Most children have their asthma under control in their daily lives – at school, at home and when they are out and about. But what about when they go away on holiday or on a school trip?

With a bit of thought and some planning, children with asthma can enjoy school trips away from home just like everyone else.

This is not a big problem. Everyone should make a checklist when they go away, to make sure they don't forget anything they need. For children with asthma it is just the same – except that **inhalers** and any other medicines should be top of the list. If the trip is abroad, they should check out the destination, too. Although it can be very cold, a holiday in the mountains would be great for someone whose asthma is brought on by house dust. House-dust mites cannot live in high places. However, city breaks could be a problem in busy areas where there are high levels of air **pollution**, as this may make asthma worse for some sufferers.

At school

Most children with asthma manage to keep it under control and their school life is unaffected. The key to keeping asthma under control at school is taking medicines at the right time. Children take their **inhalers** to school and keep them nearby at all times, or at least keep them somewhere that is easy to get at. They tell teachers and PE instructors about their asthma, so everyone is prepared in case of an **asthma attack**.

Sports

Exercise is good for all of us, and that includes those of us with asthma. The fitter you are, the better your **lungs** work. For people with asthma, this usually means they have fewer problems with their asthma. Most children with mild asthma can take part in almost any school sport or activity that they like. Some sports are especially helpful. Swimming in an indoor pool is good, because the air in the pool is warm and moist. This kind of air does not irritate sensitive **airways** as much as cold, dry air.

Team sports are good for children with asthma, too. If they have a bad day, they can always play in a position that doesn't require so much running around and still be part of the team.

Other people

Some children feel awkward about telling people
at school about their asthma. They may be
worried that they will be teased or that other
children will think they are too sick to join in
games at playtime. But most children tell
everyone they know about their asthma. After
all, it is nothing to be ashamed of and it is much
safer if people know.

*Most children
have more
interesting things
to do at school
than worry about
their asthma.*

What if people tease children with asthma, or call them names?
No one should put up with bullying. Anyone who is bullied
should tell a teacher or other adult so they can sort it out. People
who pick on someone for having asthma often don't understand
what asthma is. For example, some people wrongly think that
coughing is **contagious**, and that other children could 'catch'
asthma. Some children with asthma feel better if their teacher or
parent gives a talk to their class, or the whole school, to explain
what asthma is, and to remove any silly ideas people might have.

At home

Most of us spend a great deal of time at home. It is a safe place, but it is also where many of the **triggers** that cause asthma **symptoms** are found, such as house-dust mites and pets. For children with asthma, making changes around the home can make life much more comfortable.

House-dust mites

It is quite normal for house-dust mites to live in the dust that builds up in all our homes – in bedding, carpets, soft toys and sofas. But for many children with asthma, house-dust mites and their droppings cause a great deal of trouble. Families use various tactics to get rid of the problem.

- Washing bed covers at high temperatures once a week to kill the mites.
- Using special covers on mattresses, pillows and duvets to stop dust getting out into the room.
- Dusting rooms regularly with a damp cloth.
- Vacuuming bedrooms and beds often, using a powerful vacuum cleaner.
- Opening bedroom windows – house-dust mites are not keen on cold, dry air.

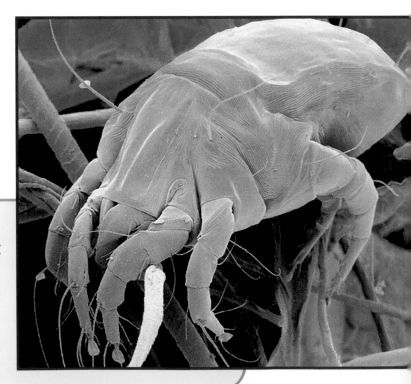

Take a look at this house-dust mite. It looks pretty horrible, but it is, in fact, only 0.3 mm long. You could not see it without the help of a microscope.

Pets

Around half the children who have asthma find that pets bring on their symptoms. Asthma **allergens** are found in pets' fur, feathers, saliva, flakes of skin and urine (wee). This means that even pets like birds can cause problems.

For most children whose asthma is brought on by contact with animals, it may be best not to have a pet at all. Some children find they can have pets, as long as they take certain precautions. They keep pets out of the lounge and bedroom, and bathe them carefully once a week.

Staying over

If you have asthma, how do you make sure you don't end up with more than just a stomach-ache from too much pizza when you sleep over at a friend's house? Other people's houses could be full of your worst asthma triggers.

- Make sure you take all necessary medicines. Warn your friend's parents what triggers the asthma and what to do in case you have an **asthma attack**.
- Make sure any furry or feathered pets are kept out of the rooms where you will sleep or spend a lot of time.
- Children with asthma should keep away from anyone who is smoking. Cigarette smoke is bad for everyone, and is a common cause of asthma attacks.

Meet Emma and Elizabeth

I'm Emma and I have asthma. I have quite long times when I don't get **asthma attacks**, and then suddenly I get quite bad asthma that lasts a few weeks. When I am wheezy I feel all out of breath and it worries me. But I am always fine when I have had a couple of puffs of my **inhaler**.

At school I sometimes need to use my inhaler at playtime, because I am running around more and that makes me wheezy. But that doesn't stop me from having fun. I used to feel a bit embarrassed if I had to use my inhaler in the classroom, because everyone kept staring at me. Now I usually do it in the corridor so no one can watch me.

Once, I stayed at my best friend Lizzie's house for four days and we went to Legoland. When we were there, towards the end of the day, I got wheezy. I tried to use my inhaler but it had run out. I was worried. We went home and Isobel (Lizzie's mum) called the doctor. Soon it was all sorted out and I had a new inhaler.

My name is Elizabeth and Emma is my best friend. My mum says Emma and I have been friends since we were babies. We're both seven and a half years old now. We do lots of things together and she often comes round to my house to sleep over at the weekends. We have a great time. When she comes she always has to bring her inhaler. That helps her breathe if her asthma gets bad. My mum keeps it somewhere safe for her.

Once when Emma came to stay with me she forgot her inhaler. We were jumping up and down on my bed and singing. Then I noticed she was feeling funny. She was wheezing. Emma got a bit scared. I told her it would be OK and gave her a little hug. Then I fetched my Mum. Mum had to get her friend to look after us while she went quickly to Emma's house and fetched Emma's inhaler. As soon as Emma got her inhaler she was better again. Most of the time, though, I don't think about Emma's asthma – she's just Emma.

Glossary

air mixture of gases that is all around us and which we breathe

airways series of tubes that carry air in and out of the lungs. The scientific name for these airways is bronchi.

allergen substance that causes an allergic reaction in some people

allergy bad reaction by the body's immune system to something in the environment

asthma attack when asthma gets out of control and some or all the symptoms of asthma appear. Asthma symptoms include wheezing, shortness of breath, coughing or a tight feeling in the chest.

bacteria tiny living things found everywhere. Some bacteria can cause diseases.

bronchi tubes that carry air in and out of the lungs

contagious a contagious disease can be passed on by touch or other contact. Asthma is not contagious, or catching.

diagnose decide what disease a person has

environment the world around us – land, sea, air, buildings and towns

hay fever allergic condition brought on by pollen. It can cause asthma symptoms.

immune system parts of the body that work together to defend it from infection and fight off diseases

inflamed red, hot or sore

inhaler device to help people with asthma breathe in their medicines

inherited when something, like eye colour or a disorder such as asthma, is passed down from parents to children

lungs parts of the body used for breathing. They are inside the chest.

mucus sticky fluid. It is made in the lungs to trap unwanted particles (tiny bits and pieces) in air so coughing can get rid of them.

oxygen a gas in the air that we breathe

peak flow meter device for measuring breathing levels. It shows how hard someone can blow air out of their lungs.

pollution something, such as fumes or smoke, that damages the environment – the air, water or land around us

prescribed when a doctor prescribes medicine, he or she says what medicine to take, and when and how much to take

preventer kind of asthma medicine that works over a long period to soothe the airways so they become less sensitive

reliever kind of asthma medicine intended to stop (relieve) the symptoms of an asthma attack quickly

respiratory to do with our breathing system

symptom sign that someone has a disease or illness. Asthma symptoms include wheezing, shortness of breath, coughing or a tight feeling in the chest.

trigger anything that irritates the airways of a person with asthma and brings on their asthma symptoms

virus tiny organism that causes diseases in animals and plants

Helpful books and addresses

BOOKS
Body Systems: Breathing, Jackie Hardie, Heinemann Library, 1996

Living with Asthma, Peta Bee, Hodder Wayland, 2000

When It's Hard to breathe, Franklin Watts

Look At Your Body: Lungs, Franklin Watts

ORGANIZATIONS AND WEBSITES
National Asthma Campaign
Junior Asthma Club
Providence House
Providence Place
London N1 ONT
Asthma Helpline Tel: 08457 010203
Website: www.asthma.org.uk

This UK charity works with people who have asthma. It has magazines covering issues concerning children with asthma, as well as the Junior Asthma Club (JAC), for young people with Asthma.

IN AUSTRALIA
National Asthma Campaign (Australia)
1 Palmerston Crescent
South Melbourne
Vic 3205
Tel: 03 9214 1476
Fax: 03 9214 1400
Email: nac@nationalasthma.org.au
Website: www.nationalasthma.org.au

Asthma Australia
National Office
Level 3/63 Stead Street
South Melbourne
Vic 3205
Freephone: 1800 645 130
Tel: 03 9696 7861
Fax: 03 9696 7397
Email: national@asthma.org.au
Website: www.asthmaaustralia.org.au

Index

allergies 8, 27
animals 8, 9, 15, 20, 21, 27
asthma attacks 4, 7, 8, 10, 14, 15, 16, 19, 21, 24, 27, 28
asthma diary 15, 18

breathing 6, 7, 10
bronchi (airways) 6, 7, 8, 11, 14, 16, 17, 24
bullying 25

check-ups 13, 18–19
chest infections 4, 10
cigarettes 9, 27
cold air 9, 15, 24
colds and flu 4, 7, 9, 20
coping with asthma 5, 14–15, 20–3
coughing 4, 7, 8, 10, 13, 15, 25

diagnosing asthma 10, 12

exercise and sports 9, 15, 21, 24

family and medical history 11

hay fever 9
holidays and school trips 23
home 26–7
house-dust mites 9, 23, 26

immune system 8
inhalers 14, 16, 17, 19, 20, 21, 23, 24, 28, 29

lungs 6, 11, 14, 18, 24

medication 7, 14, 16–17, 19–21, 23, 24
mucus 7

number of people with asthma 5

oxygen 6

peak flow meters 11, 18
pollen 9
pollution 8, 23
preventer medicines 14, 16, 17, 20

reliever medicines 14, 16, 19, 20, 21

school 24–5, 28
shortness of breath 4, 8
smoke 7, 8, 9, 27
spacers 17
symptoms 4, 7, 8, 10, 14, 16, 18, 22, 26

tight chest 4, 8, 10
treating an asthma attack 19
triggers 8, 9, 14, 15, 17, 26

viral infections 9

weather and temperature changes 9
wheezing 4, 7, 8, 10, 15, 20, 28, 29
windpipe 6

Titles in the *What does it mean to have/be* series include:

Hardback   0 431 13924 5

Hardback   0 431 13921 0

Hardback   0 431 13920 2

Hardback   0 431 13922 9

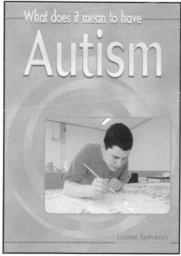

Hardback   0 431 13925 3

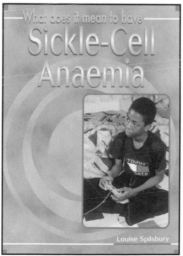

Hardback   0 431 13923 7

Find out about the other titles in this series on our website www.heinemann.co.uk/library